How-to Tips

How to Correct the Sentences

1. Read each sentence. Think about what it says.

2. Look for mistakes.

3. Fix the mistakes. You may need to add, change, or take out a word.

4. Rewrite each sentence neatly on the line. (Use another sheet of paper if you need more space.)

5. Reread your new sentence. Does it make sense and sound right?

How to Answer the Vocabulary Questions

1. Read the directions.

   - To choose a word: Read and think about each choice.

   - To figure out a word: Look for root words, affixes, or clues in a sentence.

2. Think about what you will do.

3. Reread and check your work. Does it make sense?

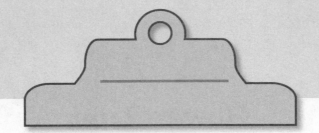

Sentence Editing Checklist

Use this checklist to help correct each sentence.

❑ Does the sentence begin with a capital letter?

❑ Does the sentence have end punctuation? (**. ? !**)

❑ Did I use capital letters to begin words that need them?
Examples:
- titles
- holidays
- geographic names

❑ Did I choose the correct word?
- homophones (to, two, too)
- verb forms (tell, told, will tell)
- pronouns (he, them, that)
- prepositions (on, above, before)
- adjectives (careful, glad), adverbs (carefully, gladly)

❑ Did I write a complete sentence?

❑ Did I put commas where they belong?
- dates (February 12, 1809)

❑ Did I put apostrophes where they belong?
- contractions (we're)
- possessives (Mary's)

Correct the sentences.

1. dolphins lives in water, but they breath air.

   _____

2. Dolphins are playfull and likes to jump flip and spin in the air

   _____

Write the missing word.

3. Dolphins live in groups, and _____ take care of each other.

   them   they

Circle the verbs.

4. When dolphins talk to each other, they squeak and whistle.

Correct the sentences.

1. Last night, I had a dreem that i lives in space.

   _____

2. I had mine own Planet that I named Marz.

   _____

Write the word that is spelled correctly.

3. An alien named Dorf was my best _____.

   freind   friend

Write the letters *ed* to form past tense verbs.

4. For fun, I **play**_____ Marzball with Dorf and **search**_____ for Marz rocks.

Correct the sentences.

1. Bats is not birds, but them fly like birds.

   _____

2. Sum people think bats is ugly and scarie.

   _____

Rewrite the sentences to make one sentence. Use the word _and_.

3. I learned that bats are gentle. Bats are helpful.

   _____

Rewrite the sentence with the correct capitalization.

4. I learned about bats in a book called <u>bats of the world</u>.

   _____

Correct the sentences.

1. Have you ever saw a rainbow after it rained

   _____

2. A rainbow happens when sun light passes through rain drops.

   _____

Write the missing root word. Use the bold word as a clue.

3. Rainbows are made up of seven **colors**. Rainbows are _____ful.

Complete the sentence. Write a word that means _full of beauty_.

4. Most people think rainbows are _____.

Read the bold prefixes and their meanings. Also notice the examples given.

Prefixes	Meanings	Examples
dis	not or opposite of	disagree
im, in	not	impossible, inactive
re	again or back	replay
un	not or opposite	untie

Write the prefix that correctly completes each bold word.

1. Dad is so sick that it is _____ **possible** for him to go to work.

2. The pizza is cold, so you need to _____ **heat** it.

3. I will not wear that shirt, because I _____ **like** the color of it.

Write as many words as you can think of using the prefixes in the box.
Try to use each prefix at least once.

4. _____   _____

  _____   _____

  _____   _____

  _____   _____

  _____   _____

Correct the sentences.

1. Before their was farms, people huntid for there food.

   _____

2. To find food, people have to live in alot of different places.

   _____

Complete the sentence with the word that is spelled correctly.

3. People stopped _____ so they could live in one place.

   moving   moveing

Complete the sentence with the best word.

4. People lived on farms and _____ their own food.

   made   grew

Correct the sentences.

1. The water on earth, is used over and over again.

   _____

2. Because new water is not made, we must save the water we had.

   _____

Underline the meaning of the bold word.

3. Water is **necessary** because it keeps living things alive.

   nice to have   needed

Write a word that means the same as *to use again*. Begin the word with the letters *re*.

4. _____

Correct the sentences.

1. Me and mom goed to the pet store on saturday.

_____

2. I wanted to look at the mouses.

_____

Complete the sentence with the word that tells when something happens.

3. _____, Mom said I could have a pet mouse.

    Recently   Outside

Complete the sentence with the correct word.

4. Today we _____ going back to the pet store to pick out a mouse.

        were   are

Correct the sentences.

1. Mom asked me what I wood like to eat for breakfest?

_____

2. I asked for Peanut butter and bannana pancakes.

_____

Complete the sentence with the word that is spelled correctly.

3. I am _____ that we have enough peanut butter.

     hopeing   hoping

Write the letters *es* to make the bold word plural.

4. I also want peanut butter **sandwich**_____ for lunch and dinner!

Read the bold suffixes and their meanings. Also notice the examples given.

Suffixes	Meanings	Examples
ful	full of	colorful
less	without	hopeless
ly	in what manner	quickly
ness	state or quality	kindness

Write the suffix that correctly completes each bold word.

1. The puppy is fun to play with because she is so **play**_____.

2. I will **glad**_____ help you with your homework.

3. Milk snakes are **harm**_____ and do not wish to hurt people.

Write as many words as you can think of using the suffixes in the box.
Try to use each suffix at least once.

4. _____   _____

   _____   _____

   _____   _____

   _____   _____

   _____   _____

Correct the sentences.

1. Tooths is what you use for biteing and chewing.

   _____

2. Some childrens start loseing baby teeth when they is six years old.

   _____

Write the missing word.

3. To take care of your teeth, use a good _____.

   hairbrush   toothbrush   scrub brush

Complete the sentence with the best word.

4. When you brush your teeth, you will also have _____ breath.

   good   fresh   nice

Correct the sentences.

1. There are people in citys who does special jobs.

   _____

2. Firefighters no how to fite fires and save peoples.

   _____

Write the word that is spelled correctly.

3. My _____ is a firefighter who helps people every day.

   nieghbor   neighbor

Complete the sentence with the best word.

4. I _____ that firefighters have an important job to do.

   think   know   believe

Correct the sentences.

1. The funnest place to go in the Summer is the city swiming pool.

_____

2. Me goes to the pool every day but if it rains.

_____

Write the correct pronoun.

3. When it rains, _____ have to stay inside.

      me   I   my

Rewrite the words to make a complete sentence. Look at number 3 for a clue.

4. it rains the pool closes.

_____

Correct the sentences.

1. Red foxxes are partly red, but they can also hav brown silver or black fur.

_____

2. The tip of a foxes tail is white, the tips of its ears are black.

_____

Complete the sentence with a preposition.

3. Foxes hunt mostly at night and sleep _____ the day.

      to enjoy   part of   during

Rewrite the sentences to make one sentence.

4. I know one fact about foxes. They have bushy tails.

_____

Read the bold homophones and their meanings.

heal	to become healthy again
heel	the back part of the foot below the ankle
he'll	the contraction for *he will*

Write the homophone that best completes each sentence.

1. Your broken arm needs time to _____, so try not to move it.

2. Dad is late for dinner, but _____ be here soon.

3. I always get a blister on my _____ when I wear a new pair of shoes.

Write a sentence using each homophone.

4. _____

    _____

    _____

Correct the sentences.

1. "I realy want to go with you at the store," I telled my freind.

_____

2. "Okay, but we has to leeve now," she sayed.

_____

Add punctuation to the sentence.

3. First I have to feed my puppy and bunnies I said

Underline the group of words that do _not_ mean exactly what they say.

4. "The store opens soon, so step on it!" she said.

Correct the sentences.

1. Does you like it when someone tels you a story

_____

2. Telling storys is some thing people has done for a long time.

_____

Complete the sentence. Write the past tense of _live_.

3. People who _____ in caves drew pictures to tell stories.

Complete the sentence with the best word.

4. When people learned to write, they _____ stories.

        spoke   wrote   painted

Correct the sentences.

1. The Holiday I like the bestest is halloween.

   _____

2. Last year I am a Dinosaur, and this year I gonna be spiderman.

   _____

Complete the sentence with the correct word.

3. My sister is going to be a green _____ with pink leaves.

                                      flower   flour

Underline the adjective in the sentence.

4. I think my sister's costume is really cute.

Correct the sentences.

1. "look at the calendar on the refrigerater," i told my little sister.

   _____

2. "What are the stikkers for," she asked.

   _____

Complete the sentence with an adverb that tells when something happens.

3. "Mom's birthday was on Monday, Dad's birthday was on Tuesday, and

   your birthday is _____."

         tomorrow   Wednesday

Write the missing word.

4. calendar : days :: clock : _____

Read the pronouns.

Subject Pronouns	Object Pronouns
I	me
she	her
we	us

Write a subject pronoun and an object pronoun to complete each sentence.

1. When Mom asked _____ to help her wash the dishes, _____ told her I would.

2. My sister gave me _____ stuffed animal, but then _____ said she wanted it back.

3. When my friends and I saw the new girl in the lunchroom, _____ asked her to sit with _____.

Write a sentence using a subject pronoun and an object pronoun from the box.

4. _____

_____

Correct the sentences.

1. I seed too butterflys in my back yard.

   _____

2. Won butterfly was red and had black spots and strips.

   _____

Complete each sentence with the word that is spelled correctly.

3. The other butterfly was _____ blue.

            plain   pleighn   playn

4. The red butterfly was pretty, but the blue butterfly was _____.

               prettyer   prettier

Correct the sentences.

1. You might think that the sun is the Planet but its not.

   _____

2. The sun is a star that is more close to earth than other stars.

   _____

Complete the bold word with the correct suffix.

3. In the **dark**_____, the other stars look like tiny dots of light.

       ness   ful   less

Underline the nouns. Explain what nouns do in a sentence.

4. Because the sun is so close to Earth, it gives us lots of light and heat.

   Explain: _____

Correct the sentences.

1. At school, were lurning about trees.

_____

2. Trees are beautifull, but they also does many importent jobs.

_____

Complete the sentence with the word that is spelled correctly.

3. The _____ on a tree keep us cool in summer.

     leafs   leaves

Complete the sentence with an adverb.

4. Trees also give us _____ tasty fruit.

     many   very

Correct the sentences.

1. i am takeing piano lessens.

_____

2. Today I learned to played a easy song.

_____

Complete the sentence with the word that is spelled correctly.

3. My teacher _____ me a song called "Old MacDonald."

     taught   teached

Complete the sentence with the correct word.

4. I was so proud of _____ when I played it for the first time.

     me   myself

Read the pronouns.

Subject Pronouns	Reflexive Pronouns
I	myself
she	herself
it	itself

Write a subject pronoun and a reflexive pronoun to complete each sentence.

1. When _____ saw _____ in the mirror,

   I saw a missing tooth.

2. The cat hurt _____ when _____ fell out
   of the tree.

3. My little sister was proud of _____ when

   _____ got a star on her drawing.

Write a sentence using a subject pronoun and a reflexive pronoun from the box.

4. _____

   _____

Correct the sentences.

1. Outside my window, I sea three cats playing on the yard.

_____

2. One of them cats is gray, and two is wite.

_____

Complete the sentence with the possessive forms of *cat*. Use apostrophes.

3. The gray _____ tail is longer than the two white _____ tails.

Underline the verbs. Explain what verbs do in a sentence.

4. The gray cat climbs a tree, and the white cats watch.

Explain: _____

Correct the sentences.

1. i weared my new shirt for Uncle Teds party.

_____

2. A boy tript and spild paint on me shirt.

_____

Complete the bold word with the prefix that means *to do again*.

3. Mom washed the shirt and then she _____**washed** it.

pre   un   re

Underline the word that has the same root as the bold word.

4. Mom was **able** to get the paint out of my shirt because it is washable.

Correct the sentences.

1. My Sister are a runner and she run races.

   _____

2. My brother is a swimer he does not race.

   _____

Complete the sentence with a word that means *one who skates*.

3. I like to skate on the ice. I want to be an ice _____.

Underline the group of words that do *not* mean exactly what they say.

4. I thought it would be hard to skate on ice, but it's a piece of cake!

Correct the sentences.

1. Menny peoples think that tomatos are vegetables.

   _____

2. A tomatoe are a fruit because it have seeds.

   _____

Complete the bold words to make them plural.

3. Tomatoes are used in **sandwich**_____, **salad**_____, and **juice**_____.

Underline the adjectives. Explain what adjectives do in a sentence.

4. I like tomatoes because they are red and juicy, and they are tasty, too.

   Explain: _____

Read the bold parts of speech and their definitions.

Parts of Speech	Definitions
noun	names a person, place, or thing
pronoun	takes the place of a noun
verb	describes an action
adjective	describes a noun
adverb	tells how, when, where, or how often

Write a word to complete each sentence. Write the name of the part of speech.

1. The red-lipped batfish has _____ lips.

   Part of speech: _____

   The ant called a panda ant looks like a panda _____.

   Part of speech: _____

   Kiwifruit is named kiwi because _____ looks like the furry brown kiwi bird.

   Part of speech: _____

   A kangaroo has powerful legs that help it _____.

   Part of speech: _____

   The tortoise moves and eats very _____.

   Part of speech: _____

Write a sentence using at least two of the parts of speech from the box.

2. _____

   _____

Correct the sentences.

1. Bobcats has short tales and thick fir.

   _____

2. Some bobcats live in forrests, and some live neer mountens.

   _____

Circle the prepositions.

3. Many bobcats live in caves or under logs.

Add _ers_ to the bold verbs. Circle to tell if the new words are verbs or nouns.

4. Bobcats are good **climb**_____ and **hunt**_____.

   verbs   nouns

Correct the sentences.

1. Its' important to keep you teeths klean and helthy.

   _____

2. Dont eat to much sugar, and brush your teeth carefuly.

   _____

Circle the pronouns.

3. There is something else you and I should do to take care of our teeth.

Complete the sentence with the correct pronoun.

4. It is also important for _____ to floss our teeth.

            we   us

Correct the sentences.

1. Tic-tac-toe are a simpel game you can play with a frend.

   _____

2. Alls you need is a pensil and a peece of paper.

   _____

Complete the sentence with the best preposition.

3. Use the pencil to draw squares _____ the paper.

   under   on

Complete the sentence with the best verb.

4. The first player _____ an **X** in a square.

   draws   creates   forms

Correct the sentences.

1. Our class room pets name is sammy

   _____

2. Sammy is brown and have a long and skinnie tail.

   _____

Write the preposition that tells about where something happens.

3. Sammy got out of his cage and ran _____ a pile of backpacks.

   underneath   during

Underline the adverb. Explain what the adverb does in the sentence.

4. I reached for Sammy and then carefully put him in his cage.

   Explain: _____

Read the bold words and their similar meanings.

> **angry**   having a strong feeling of being annoyed
>
> **grumpy**   complaining often
>
> **upset**   unhappy or worried

Choose the word that best completes each sentence.

1. I was _____ when I woke up this morning.

       grumpy   angry

2. Dad was _____ when the dog dug a hole in the yard.

       angry   grumpy

3. I know you're _____ that it's raining, but we can play a game inside.

       upset   angry

Write two sentences using two of the words from the box.

4. _____

   _____

   _____

   _____

Correct the sentences.

1. Soccer are the bestest game to play if you likes to run.

_____

2. My teem winned lots of games, but now we is done playing.

_____

Underline the noun that shows belonging.

3. Our team's name was the Bluebirds.

Write the date that is written correctly.

4. The last soccer game was on _____.

 Sunday, May 25   Sunday May, 25

Correct the sentences.

1. Have you ever seed a map of the united states

_____

2. A u.s. map show all of the States citys and rivers.

_____

Underline the meaning of the bold word.

3. Maps also show a compass with the four main **directions**.

 north, south, east, and west   words that tell how to do something

Write a word that means the same as the bold word.

4. A map can help you **locate** places you want to visit. _____

Correct the sentences.

1. The name of my favrit book are <u>judy moody</u>.

_____

2. Ive only readed the first book about judy moody.

_____

Write a word that means the opposite of the bold word.

3. On the first day of third grade, Judy is in a **bad** mood. _____

Add quotation marks to the speaker's exact words.

4. When Judy gets to her classroom, she says, Hello, Mr. Toad.

Correct the sentences.

1. There is ate planets that spinn around the sun.

_____

2. The Planet named mercury is close to the sun than Venus.

_____

Rewrite the sentences to make one sentence. Use a comma and the word _but_.

3. Mercury is very close to the sun. Mercury is not the warmest planet.

_____

Complete the sentence with the adjective that compares three or more things.

4. Mercury is the _____ planet of all eight planets.

smaller   smallest

Read the pronouns.

Subject Pronouns	Indefinite Pronouns
I	each
you	everything
we	anyone

Write a subject pronoun and an indefinite pronoun to complete each sentence.

1. _____ got two shirts for my birthday and I like

   _____ of them.

2. You must be hungry, because _____ ate

   _____ on your plate.

3. _____ lost our dog, and we don't know if

   _____ has seen her.

Write a sentence using a subject pronoun and an indefinite pronoun from the box.

4. _____

   _____

Correct the sentences.

1. I is going to vizit my grandma today.

_____

2. Grandma marys house is in a farm.

_____

Complete the sentence with the word that relates to the bold word.

3. The people who work on the **farm** are called _____.

                                    workers   farmers   helpers

Underline the words that do *not* mean exactly what they say.

4. I am going to pitch in and help feed the animals.

Correct the sentences.

1. My famly goed to florida for a vacation.

_____

2. I flied on a airplane for the first time.

_____

Underline the meaning of the bold word.

3. I got to sit in the **row** behind my mom and dad.

    to move a boat with paddles   a line of seats

Complete the sentence with an indefinite pronoun.

4. When it was time to take off, _____ had to stay seated.

                        everybody   I

Correct the sentences.

1. My teecher readed us story today.

   _____

2. The story was abowt a mouse that go to school.

   _____

Complete the bold word with the suffix that means _without_.

3. In the story, the **fear**_____ mouse visits a schoolhouse every day.

         est   ful   less

Complete the sentence with an adverb.

4. Every day, the mouse listens _____ so he can learn a lot.

         careful   carefully

Correct the sentences.

1. I and my friend Alley runned to the play ground.

   _____

2. We slided down the slide and then jumpt onto the swings.

   _____

Complete the sentence with the best adjective.

3. I felt _____ as I went higher and higher into the air.

       merry   joyful   glad

Underline the words that do _not_ mean exactly what they say.

4. My friend called out, "Take it easy! I don't want you to fall off."

Read the adjectives in each row. Notice how the adjectives change.

Adjectives	Comparative Adjectives Compare Two Things	Superlative Adjectives Compare Three or More Things
small	smaller	smallest
big	bigger	biggest
tall	taller	tallest

Write an adjective to complete each sentence.

1. The kitten is _____.

   The mouse is _____ than the kitten.

   The ant is the _____ of all.

2. A giraffe is _____.

   A building is _____ than a giraffe.

   A giant in a fairy tale is the _____ of all.

3. The car is _____.

   The bus is _____ than the car.

   The plane is the _____ of all.

Write a sentence using a comparative adjective.

4. _____

   _____

Correct the sentences.

1. Frogs spends part of their lifes under the water.

   _____

2. Frogs offen eat dragonflys cricketes and spiders.

   _____

Read the sentence to figure out the meaning of the bold word. Underline the meaning.

3. Frogs use their long, sticky tongues to **capture** food.

   to catch   to eat

4. A frog flips its tongue out, grabs the **prey**, and then eats it.

   water   an animal hunted for food

Correct the sentences.

1. Some food that is selled in stores come from far away.

   _____

2. In my town, we can by food that is growed on farms.

   _____

Complete the sentence with the word that means _nearby_.

3. The farm near my house sells food that is _____.

   colorful   tasty   local

Add the suffix _er_ to form a comparative adjective.

4. Local food can be much **fresh**_____ than food from far away.

Correct the sentences.

1. Does you no how to dance like a chicken.

   _____

2. The chicken dance is a reel dance people do evry year.

   _____

Add commas to the date.

3. Last year, Dance Like a Chicken Day was on May 14 2014.

Underline the pair of words that do *not* mean exactly what they say.

4. I was going to do the dance in class today, but I chickened out.

Correct the sentences.

1. Their are about two hunderd bones in a adults body.

   _____

2. A foot has twenty-six bones, a hand has twenty-seven bones.

   _____

Add the suffix *est* to form superlative adjectives.

3. A bone in the ear is the **small**_____ and **light**_____ bone in the body.

Complete the sentence with the correct preposition.

4. The two bones _____ the knee are called the tibia and fibula.

   beside   below

Read the bold verb phrases and their meanings.

Verb Phrases	Meanings
hand out	to give something to others
run out	to use something until it's gone
show up	to arrive at a place
watch out	to be careful

Complete each sentence with a verb phrase from the box.

1. If my friend doesn't _____ for the movie, I'll have to watch it by myself.

2. My teacher asked me to _____ pencils and paper to everybody in the class.

3. If we _____ of milk, I won't be able to eat my bowl of cereal.

4. When you ride your bike on the sidewalk, _____ for people who are walking.

Correct the sentences.

1. Some people liv in one city they whole life.

   _____

2. Some people has to mov because of its job.

   _____

Write the word that means the same as *to move to a new place*.

3. There are many reasons people _____ to new places.

                                     relocate   travel

Add a prefix to form a word that means *do not like*.

4. Many people _____**like** moving, but some people enjoy moving.

Correct the sentences.

1. You mite think werms is gross, but them are useful.

   _____

2. Farmers and People who has gardens need worms.

   _____

Complete the sentence with a word that means the same as *dirt*.

3. When worms dig tunnels, they mix the _____.

                               soil   leaves   roots

Write a subordinating conjunction to make a complete sentence.

4. _____ water and air get to the roots, the roots can grow.

Correct the sentences.

1. All fishes can here, and some can make sownds.

_____

2. They're are many kinds of noyses that fish make.

_____

Write a word that means the same as the bold word.

3. Toadfish are **able** to make noises. Toadfish _____ grunt.

Read the sentence to figure out the meaning of the bold word. Write the meaning on the line.

4. One reason toadfish grunt is to **guard** their nests.

_____

Correct the sentences.

1. The Space Needel is a tower that was builded in 1962.

_____

2. People can ride at the top of the tower in a elevater.

_____

Write a word that means the same as the bold word.

3. There is a lot to **observe** from the top of the Space Needle. _____

Write the address that is correct.

4. The Space Needle is in _____.

              Seattle, Washington   Seattle Washington

Read the bold words and their definitions.

Words	Definitions
event	something special that happens at a certain time and place
task	a job that needs to be done
effect	the result of an action
feature	a part of something

Draw lines to match.

1. event   itchy skin after a bee stings you

   task   the nose on your face

   effect   a birthday party

   feature   sweeping the floor

Write a sentence using one of the bold words from the box.

2. _____

_____

Correct the sentences.

1. Honeybees is insects who make hunny.

   _____

2. Honeybees has five eyes, they see only a few colers.

   _____

Rewrite the sentences to make one sentence. Use a comma and the coordinating conjunction *and*.

3. Honeybees live in hives. Their hives are made of wax.

   _____

Write a word that means the same as the bold word.

4. The bees **collect** nectar and make honey out of it. _____

Correct the sentences.

1. Fossils teach us about animuls weve never seen.

   _____

2. We know about dinosaurs because of its fossils.

   _____

Complete the sentence with the best word or words.

3. When lots of sand covers an animal and gets hard, a fossil _____.

                                           appears   forms   shows up

Complete the bold word with the prefix that means *again*.

4. Scientists can put fossils together to _____-**create** the shape of a dinosaur.

Correct the sentences.

1. There are for seesons in a year.

_____

2. Summer is warm than spring, and winter is cold than fall.

_____

Complete the sentence with the best word.

3. Summer _____ during the months of June, July, and August.

     happens   comes   occurs

Write a complete sentence. Begin the sentence with the subordinating conjunction _when_.

4. It's winter in the U.S., it's summer in another part of the world.

_____

Correct the sentences.

1. Today my famly visited the sity animal shelter.

_____

2. In a korner of the room, i saw a brown cat in a caje.

_____

Write a prefix to form a word that means _not usual_.

3. It had a long body and red eyes. It was the most _____**usual** cat
I'd ever seen.

Add quotation marks to show a person's exact words. Add a comma after the word _said_.

4. Dad looked in the cage, and then he said That's not a cat!

Read the pairs of possessive pronouns and possessive adjectives.
Notice the difference between them.

Possessive Pronouns	Possessive Adjectives
mine	my
hers	her
yours	your

Write a pronoun/adjective pair from the box to complete each sentence.

1. _____ backpack is on the porch, but the book beside

   it is not _____.

2. I told my friend that I like _____ hat, but she said that

   the hat is not _____.

3. Is this book _____, or is _____ book
   on the shelf?

Write a sentence using a possessive pronoun and a possessive adjective from the box.

4. _____

   _____

Correct the sentences.

1. butterflys and moths are diffrent in some ways.

_____

2. Most butterflys flys during day, and most moths fly at nite.

_____

Underline the adjectives. Explain what adjectives do in a sentence.

3. Moths that fly at night have thick, fuzzy bodies and dull colors.

Explain: _____

Complete the sentence with an adjective.

4. Many butterflies have _____ bright colors on their wings.

                             several   really

Correct the sentences.

1. Theres a T. rex named Sue in chicago illinois.

_____

2. Sues bones are in a museum called the field museum.

_____

Write a word that means the same as the bold word.

3. Sue Hendrickson **discovered** the bones of the T. rex. _____

Underline the verb in the sentence. Explain what verbs do in a sentence.

4. Sue Hendrickson found Sue's bones near the city of Faith, South Dakota.

Explain: _____

Correct the sentences.

1. "What are we haveing for dinner" I asked Mom?

_____

2. "Im makeing pan cakes" Mom said.

_____

Label the pronouns as *subject* and *indefinite*.

3. "I'm going to let **everyone** pick two toppings," **she** added.

_____ _____

Complete the sentence with the word that is spelled correctly.

4. "I want sliced bananas and _____ nuts," I said.

                 choped   chopped   chopt

Correct the sentences.

1. George washington becomed president of United States in 1789.

_____

2. Washington D.C., is named after mr. Washington

_____

Complete the sentence with the word that is spelled correctly.

3. There is a _____ about George chopping down a cherry tree.

       folk tale   folk tail

Underline the nouns.

4. People in America remember George Washington as a great man.

Read each row of phrases. Notice how the phrases say the same thing but in different ways.

Means exactly what the words say	Does *not* mean exactly what the words say
He is scared.	He has cold feet.
I don't feel good.	I am under the weather.
Help me.	Give me a hand.
Wait!	Hold your horses!

Complete each sentence with a phrase that means exactly what the words say.

1. I have to stay in bed today because _____.

2. He doesn't want to ride the roller coaster because _____.

Complete each sentence with a phrase that does *not* mean exactly what the words say.

3. I can't go with you until I finish my lunch, so _____.

4. Will you _____ with my homework?

Correct the sentences.

1. Today i lernt a lot, about the state of virginia.

   _____

2. Virginia's song is called "carry me back to old Virginia"

   _____

Complete the sentence with the plural word that is spelled correctly.

3. Virginia was one of the thirteen original _____.

                                   colonies   colonys   collinies

Add apostrophes to make possessive nouns.

4. Virginia is George Washingtons home state and Thomas Jeffersons home state.

Correct the sentences.

1. Weels and forks are to simpel machines.

   _____

2. simple machines make work easyer for people.

   _____

Complete the bold words to form plural nouns.

3. Rakes pick up **lea**_____, and **kni**_____ cut food.

Underline the possessive pronoun. Circle the possessive adjective.

4. One simple machine of mine is my scissors.

Correct the sentences.

1. Lemonade is a drink that is maked with lemmons.

_____

2. My friends and me sell lemonade during the summer.

_____

Read the sentence to figure out the meaning of the bold word. Write the meaning on the line.

3. People can **purchase** a glass of lemonade for ten cents.

_____

Underline the words that have the same root.

4. People enjoy drinking lemonade. Selling lemonade is enjoyable.

Correct the sentences.

1. I likes to kullect rocks where ever I go.

_____

2. I find them rocks in lots of plases.

_____

Write prepositions to complete the sentence.

3. Today when I was _____ the beach, I found a rock stuck _____ the mud.

Rewrite the sentences to make one sentence.

4. When I got home, I cleaned the rock. I put it in a box.

_____

Read each row of nouns. Notice how the nouns are different.

Regular Nouns (person, place, or thing)	Abstract Nouns (cannot see, hear, smell, touch, or taste)
animals	kindness
flag	respect
president	honesty

Complete each sentence with a pair of nouns from above.

1. One famous _____ was known for his

   _____.

2. The animal doctor treats the _____ with

   _____.

3. The American _____ is something people

   _____.

Write two abstract nouns.

4. _____

   _____

Correct the sentences.

1. Pumpkins is a frute becuz they have seeds.

_____

2. Long ago, Native americans use the seeds for food.

_____

Complete the sentence with a preposition.

3. There are about 500 seeds _____ a pumpkin.

Complete the sentence with the word that is spelled correctly.

4. After the seeds are _____ out, you can make a jack-o-lantern.

       taked   tooken   taken

Correct the sentences.

1. Lady bugs are insects cald beetles.

_____

2. Ladybugs live in feelds forests and gardens.

_____

Add the letters _ly_ to the bold word. Circle the part of speech of the new word.

3. Most ladybugs have **bright**_____ colored bodies with black spots.

   adjective   adverb

Rewrite the sentences to make one sentence. Use the coordinating conjunction _because_.

4. Ladybugs hide during the winter. They don't like to be cold.

_____

Correct the sentences.

1. orville and wilbur wright was brothers.

_____

2. The too brothers dreemed about flying.

_____

Complete the sentence with a possessive pronoun.

3. They knew that the flying machine would be an invention of _____.

Complete the sentence with the best word.

4. In 1903, the brothers _____ in the airplane they invented.

                         flew   rode

Correct the sentences.

1. Penguins had black and white fethers.

_____

2. Penguins can not fly but they swim real fast.

_____

Complete the sentence with a possessive pronoun.

3. A penguin moves quickly on land by hopping on both of _____ feet.

Write the best word to complete the sentence.

4. Penguins like to _____ across the ice on their tummies.

                slide   skip   skate

Read the bold words and their definitions.

Words	Definitions
authority	a person who is in charge
concentrate	to carefully study something; to pay careful attention
revise	to make corrections or rewrite something
fact	something that is known to be true

Write about a time you listened to someone who is an authority.

1. _____

_____

Write about a time when you had to concentrate.

2. _____

_____

Write about a time when you revised something you wrote.

3. _____

_____

Write about a fact that you know.

4. _____

_____

Correct the sentences.

1. Johnny appleseeds real name was john chapman.

_____

2. Johnny plantid apple seeds every where he goed.

_____

Underline the words that have the same root.

3. Johnny carefully planted the seeds, and he cared for the land.

Underline the abstract nouns.

4. Johnny Appleseed was known for his kindness and gentleness.

Correct the sentences.

1. Jelly beens are small colorful and yummy candys.

_____

2. People has injoyed jelly beans for long time.

_____

Complete the sentence with the word that is spelled correctly.

3. Long ago, people _____ jelly beans for a few pennies.
         buyed   bought   bott

Read the sentences to figure out the meaning of the bold word. Underline the meaning.

4. The jelly beans in a bag were all one color. Now the colors are **combined**.

    colorful   mixed together

Correct the sentences.

1. "Why are this dogs barking so loud," I asked my dad.

   _____

2. "They sea our cat sitting on the fense?" he said.

   _____

Underline the speaker's words. Explain how you know they are the speaker's words.

3. "Let's take Fluffy inside," I whispered.

   _____

Complete the analogy.

4. loud : loudly :: quiet : _____

Correct the sentences.

1. I am gonna wash Moms car.

   _____

2. I'll need sope, a bucket, and sponge.

   _____

Complete the sentence with an adverb that tells when something happens.

3. I'll wash the top and sides first, and I'll wash the tires _____.

                                                     next   outside

Complete the sentence with the best word.

4. Mom said to _____ the tires because they are very dirty.

        pat   scrub   wipe

Read the verb phrases and their meanings.

Verb Phrases	Meanings
look after	to take care of
figure out	to decide
get along	to be friendly with; to work well together
dress up	to wear fancy clothes

Complete each sentence with a bold verb phrase from the box.

1. I like to read before I go to bed, but sometimes it's hard to

   _____ what book to read.

2. Mom said that I have to _____ for my grandma's
   birthday party.

3. When Dad is busy making dinner, I _____ my little
   sister.

4. When my brother and I argue, Mom tells us to _____.

Correct the sentences.

1. Mom is too bizy to made dinner.

   _____

2. Dad and me are going to make dinner.

   _____

Write the word *will* to form the future verb tense.

3. We _____ shop for food, and then we _____ cook it.

Add a prefix to form a word that means *to heat again*.

4. When Mom gets home, we will _____**heat** her dinner.

Correct the sentences.

1. An tall tail is a story about a speshul hero.

   _____

2. The hero is usual tall and strong than anyone in real life.

   _____

Complete the sentence with the best word.

3. Heroes in tall tales do things that are hard to _____.

   know   believe   think

Make a complex sentence. Use the subordinating conjunction *When*.

4. _____ Paul Bunyan rolled over in his sleep, he caused

   an earthquake.

Correct the sentences.

1. Snails has soft bodys and hard shels.

   _____

2. A snails shell protects their body.

   _____

Complete the sentence with adjectives.

3. A snail's body is _____ and _____.

   long   near   slimy   outside

Rewrite the sentences to make one sentence. Use the coordinating conjunction *because*.

4. Snails are active at night. They don't like sunshine.

   _____

Correct the sentences.

1. "Whats that sound your making? I asked my friend.

   _____

2. "I have the hiccups i can't stop," she said.

   _____

Add a comma to make a compound sentence.

3. "Stick your fingers in your ears then sip some water," I told her.

Complete the sentence with the best word.

4. "I hate the hiccups, so I _____ it works," she said.

   expect   hope   wish

Read the adverbs in each row. Notice how the adverbs change.

Adverbs	Comparative Adverbs Compare Two Things	Superlative Adverbs Compare Three or More Things
hard	harder	hardest
carefully	more carefully	most carefully
often	more often	most often

Write an adverb or adverb phrase to complete each sentence.

1. I work _____ to get good grades.

   You work _____ than I do.

   They work the _____ of anyone in the class.

2. I carry my tray of food _____.

   You carry your tray of food _____ than I do.

   They carry their trays of food the _____ of anyone in the lunchroom.

3. I watch movies _____.

   You watch movies _____ than I do.

   They watch movies the _____ of anyone in our neighborhood.

Write a sentence using the superlative form of an adverb.

4. _____

   _____

Correct the sentences.

1. jiraffes have long tungs necks and legs.

   _____

2. Their legs are tall than many people.

   _____

Complete the sentence with the correct homophone.

3. Giraffes have the longest _____ of any animal on land.

   tail   tale

Write a pronoun that agrees with the bold noun.

4. A **giraffe** has to spread _____ legs and bend down to drink.

Correct the sentences.

1. Abraham lincoln was born on February 12 1809

   _____

2. Another name for Mr. Lincoln was honest abe.

   _____

Complete the sentence with an abstract noun.

3. Abe Lincoln was known for his belief in _____ for all people.

   freedom   beards   hats

Read the sentence to figure out the meaning of the bold word. Underline the meaning.

4. Lincoln used his hat to **store** money and important papers.

   a place that sells items   to keep for later use

Correct the sentences.

1. I meeted the new boy in are class.

_____

2. Him movd here from another kountry.

_____

Label the bold pronouns as *subject* or *reflexive*.

3. When **he** came to America, he taught **himself** how to speak English.

_____   _____

Underline the words that do *not* mean exactly what they say.

4. I'm tickled pink that I made a new friend.

Correct the sentences.

1. My grand father is a grate man.

_____

2. I write a poem for he called "my grandpa and me."

_____

Complete the sentence with an adjective.

3. In the poem, I described Grandpa as a _____ man.

        gently   gentle

Complete the sentence with the best word.

4. I used the word *sunny* to _____ with *funny*.

        compare   rhyme

Read the words.

> sick   answer   tidy
>
> mend   sleep   messy

Write the synonym.

1. **repair** _____   **slumber** _____

   neat _____   **sloppy** _____

   ill _____   **reply** _____

Complete each sentence with synonyms.

2. I make sure that my room is _____ before I go to bed because

   I sleep better in a _____ room.

3. I hope I'm not getting _____, because my mom said I can't

   go to the party if I'm _____.

4. Bears _____ in winter because it's cold, there's little food

   to eat, and there's nothing else to do but _____.

Correct the sentences.

1. Christopher Columbus was an explorer who spended a lot of time at see.

   _____

2. Columbus wantid to find a more quick way to get to Asia.

   _____

Complete the sentence with the best word or words.

3. The king and queen of Spain gave Columbus the money and ships he

   needed for _____.
         studying   exploring   making maps

Complete the bold word to form a past tense verb.

4. In 1492, Columbus **journ**_____ across the Atlantic Ocean.

Correct the sentences.

1. Jerms are finded in plases that is dirty.

   _____

2. Germs can get inside peoples bodys and make em sick.

   _____

Add a comma to make a complex sentence.

3. Since germs are found on food we should wash food before we eat it.

Underline the words that have the same root.

4. People should always wash their hands after they handle food.

Correct the sentences.

1. I lik being in third grad.

   _____

2. My teecher make it fun for the holl class.

   _____

Complete the sentence.

3. Anyone who turns in _____ homework gets a sticker.

                          their   his or her

Rewrite the sentence to make two sentences.

4. Fridays are really fun because we get to play games.

   _____

Correct the sentences.

1. A Map tell you wear places are.

   _____

2. A map can be a pitcher of your school, a town, or world.

   _____

Are the bold words synonyms or antonyms? Write the answer on the line.

3. Using a map is a **way** to find places. It's a **method** of knowing which way to go.

   _____

Write a synonym for the bold word.

4. A map is very helpful if you go on a **journey**. _____

Read the words.

> fix   shallow   lead
>
> polite   full   tame

Write the antonym.

1. **empty** _____   **deep** _____

   follow _____   **rude** _____

   wild _____   **break** _____

Complete each sentence with antonyms.

2. When my little sister and I go swimming, she stays in the

   _____ end of the pool, and I swim in the

   _____ end.

3. This morning, my brother's toy box was _____, but he took

   out all the toys and now it is _____.

4. "I need one student to be in front to _____ the parade, and

   I need the rest of you to _____ the leader," my teacher said.

Correct the sentences.

1. Martin Luther King, Jr., was born in Atlanta Georgia on January 15 1929,

_____

2. Dr. king believt that all people should be eqwal.

_____

Underline the possessive pronoun.

3. He is famous for his speech that begins, "I have a dream."

Make the adjective _fair_ an adverb.

4. Dr. King wanted all people to be treated **fair**_____.

Correct the sentences.

1. sweet potatos is not potatos.

_____

2. Sweet potatoes are more easy to grow than potatoes

_____

Underline the adjectives.

3. The skin of a sweet potato is smooth and can be white, red, golden, or purple.

Write a synonym for the bold word.

4. China **produces** most of the sweet potatoes in the world.

_____

Correct the sentences.

1. I brush my tooths everyday.

   _____

2. I doesn't want cavities, when I go to the dentist.

   _____

Complete the bold words to form comparative adjectives.

3. A cavity is a hole that can grow **big**_____ and **deep**_____.

Read the sentence to figure out the meaning of the bold word. Underline the meaning.

4. Brushing and flossing every day will help **prevent** cavities.

   to keep from happening   to make happen

Correct the sentences.

1. "Did you had a good day at school," mom asked.

   _____

2. "I learnt how to play a new game," I telled her.

   _____

Add punctuation to the sentence.

3. We turned cards over to find a match I said.

Add punctuation to make two sentences.

4. "That sounds like the game Memory I love that game!" she said.

Read the definitions.

> a. to tell about something;
>   to give details
>
> b. to lead
>
> c. to go somewhere with
>   someone
>
> d. to happen
>
> e. knowing something
>
> f. to give words of comfort

Write the letter of the definition of each bold word.

1. **describe** _____   **accompany** _____   **aware** _____

   assure _____   **occur** _____   **conduct** _____

Write three sentences using three words from number 1.

2. _____

   _____

3. _____

   _____

4. _____

   _____

Correct the sentences.

1. I was getting reddy to go at the park.

   _____

2. Mom said i could'nt go if it rain.

   _____

Underline the words that do *not* mean exactly what they say.

3. When it started to rain, I was down in the dumps.

Complete the sentence with the best word.

4. For most of the day, I _____ sadly out the window.

           stared   peeked   glanced

Correct the sentences.

1. Wunce there be a boy who lived in a village.

   _____

2. The boy was board, so he cryed out, "a wolf is chasing the sheep!"

   _____

Write the meaning of the bold word.

3. When the **villagers** came to chase the wolf away, they did not see a wolf.

   _____

Complete the sentence with the best word.

4. The boy had lied. He had not been _____.

           correct   truthful   certain

Correct the sentences.

1. When water in the air freeze, it can turn into sno.

   _____

2. Even tho snows very cold, many people injoy it.

   _____

Complete the bold word with the suffix that means _without_.

3. Snowflakes are not white. They are clear and **color**_____.

   ful   less

Complete the sentence with a subordinating conjunction.

4. _____ all snowflakes have six sides, each one looks different.

   And   Although   But

Correct the sentences.

1. I have heared about sqirrels that can fly.

   _____

2. Them have large, flat tails that help them mov.

   _____

Complete the sentence with the best preposition.

3. Flying squirrels travel _____ trees.

   under   between   into

Complete the sentence with the best word.

4. Squirrels don't actually fly, but they do _____ through the air.

   slide   swim   glide

Read the bold irregular verbs and their definitions.

Irregular Verbs	Definitions
lay **laying**	to put something down
lie **lying**	to rest on something flat such as a floor

Complete each sentence with the correct irregular verb.

1. Pick up the trash that is _____ on the floor.

2. Please _____ the book on the table.

3. I like to _____ on the beach when it's sunny.

Write a sentence that uses one irregular verb from above.

4. _____

_____

Correct the sentences.

1. Horses eyes are on the sides of its head.

_____

2. A horses teeth take up more space than their brain.

_____

Underline the adverbs. Write what the adverbs tell about: when or where.

3. After a horse is born, it is soon able to run.   _____

Complete the sentence with the correct irregular verb.

4. Horses can sleep both _____ down and standing up.

　　　　　　　　　laying　　　　lying

Correct the sentences.

1. Peanuts are mor like beens then nuts.

_____

2. Four main tipes of peanuts is growed in the U.S.

_____

Underline the meaning of the bold word.

3. Two peanut farmers were **elected** president of the United States.

　　asked to be　　　　chosen or voted to be

Complete the bold word with a suffix that means *one who*.

4. China is the world's largest **produc**_____ of peanuts.

Correct the sentences.

1. The giant sqwid has the larger eyes in the world.

_____

2. The first music CD made in the U.S. was "born in the usa"

_____

Complete the bold word with the prefix that means *not*.

3. It is almost _____**possible** for people to tickle themselves.

        im   pre

Complete the sentence with the contraction for *cannot*.

4. A crocodile _____ stick its tongue out.

Correct the sentences.

1. the grand canyon was formd by the colorado River.

_____

2. The water in the River carryd away rocks and dirt.

_____

Add a suffix to form comparative adjectives.

3. The water was like a knife. It cut deep_____ and deep_____ into the earth.

Underline the meaning of the verb phrase.

4. When water and wind **wear away** Earth's surface, a canyon is formed.

   to make something appear   to make something disappear

Read the sentences. Think about what it's like to go camping.

> Camping is fun.
>
> I like to <u>hike</u> on <u>trails</u>.
>
> I carry a <u>backpack</u>.
>
> We sit on <u>logs</u> around the campfire.
>
> At night, I sleep in a <u>tent</u>.
>
> I use a <u>flashlight</u> to read a book.

Read each bold word. Then write a similar word you would use to tell about camping. Use the underlined words from above.

1. **walk** _____   **chairs** _____

   purse _____   **lamp** _____

   roads _____   **room** _____

Write the word or words that tell about camping.

2. It's cold in the forest, but I am warm and cozy in my _____.

   sleeping bag   bed

3. When I hike up the hill, I wear my hiking _____.

   slippers   boots

Write a sentence about camping. Use at least two of the underlined words from the box.

4. _____

   _____

Correct the sentences.

1. Mark Twain was a fameous writor.

   _____

2. Mark Twain writed the book <u>the adventures of tom sawyer</u>.

   _____

Write the past tense of the word _dream_.

3. When Mark Twain was a boy, he _____ about working on a steamboat.

Underline the abstract noun.

4. Mark Twain's dream of working on a steamboat came true.

Correct the sentences.

1. People who invent things are call inventers.

   _____

2. Thomas Edison inventid menny things.

   _____

Underline the two words that have the same root.

3. Thomas Edison worked with electricity to make an electric light bulb.

Underline the meaning of the bold word.

4. Edison didn't invent the light bulb, but he made many changes to **improve** it.

   make it better   sell it

Correct the sentences.

1. The first machine that was builded to wash dishes was woodin.

_____

2. People used a handel to turn a weel.

_____

Complete the sentence with the best word.

3. The wheel _____ water on the dishes.

　　spit　　　sprinkled　　　splashed

Complete the analogy.

4. useless : not practical :: useful : _____

Correct the sentences.

1. The planet kalled saturn have rings.

_____

2. The planets rings are made of ise, dust, and rock.

_____

Write a prefix to make a word that means the opposite of the bold word.

3. Sometimes Saturn's rings **appear**, and sometimes they _____appear.

Complete the sentence with the adverb that tells where something happens.

4. Saturn has six main rings with space in _____.

　　　　　　　　　　　　between　　　before

Read each row of phrases. Notice how the phrases say the same thing but in different ways.

Means exactly what the words say	Does *not* mean exactly what the words say
You were right.	You hit the nail on the head.
I'm very happy.	I'm on cloud nine.
She can grow plants well.	She has a green thumb.
I'm feeling unhappy.	I'm feeling blue.

Complete each sentence with a phrase that means exactly what the words say.

1. I got a new bike for my birthday, and that's why _____

   _____.

2. _____ because my best

   friend moved away.

Complete each sentence with a phrase that does *not* mean exactly what the words say.

3. When you said it was going to rain today, _____

   _____.

4. Mrs. Johnson's garden is so beautiful, people say _____

   _____.

Correct the sentences.

1. Krickets make a chirping nois.

   _____

2. Them rubb there wings together.

   _____

Circle the word that is closest in meaning to the bold word.

3. Warm weather gives crickets the **power** to chirp.

   energy   idea   need

Write the word that best completes the sentence.

4. Although I can't prove it, I _____ that crickets are good luck.

   understand   know   believe

Correct the sentences.

1. Hot whether can make our bodys sweat.

   _____

2. Sweat make a body more cool.

   _____

Complete the sentence with the correct homophone.

3. The _____ reason people sweat is heat.
   main   mane   Maine

Underline the preposition that tells when something happens.

4. When you play outside in the heat, drink lots of water during the day.

Correct the sentences.

1. The first bikes maded did not have peddals.

_____

2. The wheels on the first bicicles were not same size.

_____

Write an antonym for the bold word.

3. Bicycles today have two wheels that are the **same** size. _____

Complete the analogy.

4. bicycle : two :: tricycle : _____

Correct the sentences.

1. Washington becomed a state on November 11 1889.

_____

2. in 1889, Washington didnt have a flag of it's own.

_____

Label each bold word with the correct meaning: *people in charge* or *approved*.

3. The **officials** in Washington did not choose an **official** flag until 1923.

_____   _____

Underline the meaning of the bold word.

4. The flag is the only state flag that **displays** a picture of a president.

    hides   shows

Read the word root and its meaning in the shaded box. Then read the bold words and their definitions.

vis means *see*	
visit	to go to see and spend time with
television	an object with a screen that shows moving pictures and makes sounds
invisible	not able to be seen

Write the word from the box that best completes each sentence.

1. I see the trees blowing outside my window, but I can't see the wind because

   it is _____.

2. I want to see my grandma, so I will _____ her on Sunday.

3. I can't wait to see my favorite show on our brand new _____.

Write a sentence using one of the bold words from the box.

4. _____

   _____

Correct the sentences.

1. Befor their was money people, used food and animals to bye things.

   _____

2. If a man had a cow, they could trade it for bag of wheat.

   _____

Add a comma to make a complex sentence.

3. Since cows were not easy to carry around people made metal coins.

Write the comparative form of the adverb *easily*.

4. Coins could be carried _____ than animals and lasted a long time.

Correct the sentences.

1. Mine family went to South, Dakota last summur.

   _____

2. At dinosaur park in rapid city, I seen jiant dinosaurs.

   _____

Read the sentence to figure out the meaning of the bold word. Underline the meaning.

3. The dinosaurs were huge **figures** that looked like cartoon characters.

   statues   numbers

Complete the sentence with a possessive pronoun.

4. Dinosaurs are a favorite subject of _____.

Correct the sentences.

1. Raindeer grow very quick after they is born.

_____

2. Reindeers travel together to surch for food.

_____

Complete the sentence with an adverb.

3. Reindeer's food is often hidden under the snow, but they can

_____ smell it.

    easy   easily

Complete the sentence with the best word.

4. Reindeer use their _____ to dig down through the snow.

    hooves   feet   shoes

Correct the sentences.

1. Do you know how bubbel gum and chewing gum are diffrent?

_____

2. Bubble gum is thiker then chewing gum.

_____

Underline the two words that are related.

3. Because bubble gum has the ability to stretch, I'm able to blow bubbles with it.

Underline the words that have similar meanings. Write _synonyms_ or _antonyms_.

4. Bubble gum is usually pink, and chewing gum is often gray.

_____

Read the bold words and their similar meanings.

able	having the power to do something
skillful	having or showing skill
trained	taught how to do a job

Write the word that best completes each sentence.

1. The artist is very _____ at painting pictures.

2. I am _____ to walk you to school today.

3. My favorite act at the zoo is the _____ seal.

Write two sentences using two of the words from the box.

4. _____

_____

_____

_____

Correct the sentences.

1. the liberty bell is in Philadelphia Pennsylvania.

_____

2. The bell ringed in 1776 when the declaration of independence was readed.

_____

Write the word that correctly completes the sentence.

3. The first bell that was made cracked because _____ metal was too thin.

                                                      its   it's

Underline the pair of words that do *not* mean exactly what they say.

4. The bell means a lot to Americans because it stands for freedom.

Correct the sentences.

1. If your school have a team, those team might has a mascot.

_____

2. A mascot is a person who dress up like a karacter.

_____

Underline the words that do *not* mean exactly what they say.

3. Mascots act like they have ants in their pants.

Underline the word that has a root that means *to move*.

4. Mascots move around a lot, and their motions can make people laugh.

Correct the sentences.

1. The human brane is like a compewter.

_____

2. Are brane controls how us think and act.

_____

Underline the words that have the same root.

3. The brain also controls our memories and allows us to remember things.

Underline the meaning of the bold word.

4. Your brain helps you **decide** what to wear on a rainy day.

   to make a choice about something   to forget

Correct the sentences.

1. A cat's hearing is more better than a dogs hearing.

_____

2. The sense of hearing is a cat's goodest sense.

_____

Write an antonym for the bold word.

3. Cats have a **powerful** sense of smell, too. _____

Complete the sentence with the correct homophone.

4. If a cat smells the _____ of another cat, it might get upset.

     sent   scent   cent

Read the prepositions.

to	by	over	with
at	across	in	on

Write the preposition or prepositions that best complete each sentence.

1. To get to the other side of the lake, row your boat _____ the water.

2. He hit the ball so hard, it flew _____ the fence.

3. When Mom and Dad are _____ work, I am

   _____ my classroom at school.

Write sentences using three prepositions from above.

4. _____

   _____

   _____

   _____

   _____

Correct the sentences.

1. "Is a sea lyon and a seel the same," I asked my teacher.

_____

2. "Them are two different animals, her said.

_____

Complete the sentences with prepositions.

3. "Sea lions can walk _____ land using their long flippers. Seals can only

   move well _____ the water."

Add punctuation to the sentence.

4. She said Sea lions bark loudly, but seals only grunt

Correct the sentences.

1. Alot of people like to rite in a diary.

_____

2. People like to write about what happens in his or her lifes.

_____

Is the bold word a possessive pronoun or a possessive adjective? Underline the answer.

3. A diary is a good place to write the thoughts and feelings that are only **yours**.

   possessive pronoun   possessive adjective

Complete the sentence with the best word.

4. Another word for a diary is _____.

   book   journal   calendar

Correct the sentences.

1. "Whats a shadow"? my little sister asked me.

   _____

2. "Turn off the light and I'll show you, I told her."

   _____

Rewrite the words to make a complete sentence. Use a coordinating conjunction.

3. "Turn on the flashlight point it at the wall," I said.

   _____

Write a word to make a complex sentence.

4. "_____ make a shadow, hold your hand between the flashlight and the wall."

Correct the sentences.

1. makeing food inside a oven is called bakeing.

   _____

2. Some food that are bakt are brownies cake and pizza

   _____

Write the suffixes to correctly complete the bold words.

3. A person called a **bak**_____ works in a **bak**_____ and **bak**_____ bread.

       es   ery   er

Complete the sentence with the best word.

4. Bakers measure ingredients carefully. They don't _____.

                         wonder   pretend   guess

Read the words.

collection   location

shiny   careful

Complete each sentence with a word that has the same root as the bold word.

1. I like to **collect** rocks, so my teacher suggested that I start a rock

   _____.

2. When Rudolph's nose **shines**, it makes a _____ red light.

3. Mom and Dad **care** about me and my sister, so they always tell us

   to be _____.

4. When I asked the store clerk to help me **locate** a box of Tasty O's, she

   showed me the _____ of the cereal.

Correct the sentences.

1. A pond is not the same as a lak, streem, or river.

   _____

2. A pond is small, it is home to lots of animals and plants.

   _____

Underline the two words that have the same root.

3. Living things are able to grow because pond plants are capable of making

   food and air.

Read the sentence to figure out the meaning of the bold word. Underline the meaning.

4. The plants that rise up out of the water offer **shelter** to the animals.

   privacy   protection

Correct the sentences.

1. A lighthouse is a towur that has a lite at the top.

   _____

2. The perpose of a lighthouse is to make brite light that ships can sea.

   _____

Underline the adjectives in the sentence.

3. A lighthouse guides ships through bad weather, thick fog, and dark nights.

Write an antonym for the bold word.

4. Lighthouses **reduce** the chances that a ship will crash. _____

Correct the sentences.

1. Fireflies aint flys or bugs.

   _____

2. Fireflies are beetels that flew.

   _____

Underline the words that make the superlative form of the adjective *noticeable*.

3. The yellow, green, and orange lights that fireflies make are most noticeable during summer nights.

Complete the sentence with an adverb.

4. At night, fireflies on a tree can look like a _____ lit Christmas tree.

   brightly   bright

Correct the sentences.

1. The explorers who first finded pineapples thinked them were pinecones.

   _____

2. Pineapples were carryed around the World on saleing ships.

   _____

Complete the sentence.

3. Besides fresh pineapple and pineapple juice, there is canned pineapple,

   which comes in a _____.

Complete the sentence with an adverb.

4. Some people think that it's best to eat pineapple _____.

   fresh   daily

Read the words.

> comfort   comfortable   uncomfortable

Write the word that best completes each sentence.

1. Goldilocks was very _____ in Baby Bear's soft, warm bed.

2. Mom and Dad _____ me whenever I have a bad dream.

3. The cold metal chairs in the library are very _____.

Write the word part or parts that changed the meaning of _comfort_.

4. comfortable:

_____

uncomfortable:

_____

Correct the sentences.

1. It taked nine years for workors to build the statue of liberty.

   _____

2. the statue was finished, it was gived to America on July 4 1884.

   _____

Read the sentence to figure out the meaning of the bold word. Underline the meaning.

3. The Statue of Liberty was a **present** to the U.S. from France.

   a gift   the period of time happening now

Complete the analogy.

4. July 4 : date :: two o'clock : _____

Correct the sentences.

1. On October 25 1881, Pablo Picasso was born.

   _____

2. Picasso was an artest who painted his first picture when him was nine.

   _____

Rewrite the sentences to make a simple sentence.

3. Picasso went to an art school. He went to art school in Spain.

   _____

Add punctuation to the sentence.

4. Pablo Picasso once said Everything you can imagine is real

Correct the sentences.

1. Some one who is a docter for animals is called a veterinarian.

   _____

2. When a animal is sick, the doctor checks them to find out what's rong.

   _____

Write the meaning of the bold word.

3. To **prevent** animals from getting sick, doctors give them shots.

   _____

Underline the adverb. Circle the adjective.

4. Pets should go to a doctor regularly for regular checkups.

Correct the sentences.

1. Water kovers more then haf of Earth

   _____

2. Our planet look blue from space there is so much water.

   _____

Write a prefix to make a word that means *not drinkable*.

3. Most of Earth's water is _____drinkable.

Underline the group of words that contain the same root as the bold word.

4. The **majority** of the world's water is salt water.

   the major part   the biggest part

Read the words.

> basket   squash
>
> bill   coat

Read each pair of clues. Write a word from the box that goes with the clues.

1. a vegetable   what you do to a bug   _____

   holds laundry   used to carry Easter eggs   _____

   an animal's fur   what you wear in winter   _____

   a bird's beak   a boy's name   _____

Write a pair of words that have more than one meaning.

2. _____   _____

Write a sentence using each of the words you wrote.

3. _____

   _____

4. _____

   _____

Correct the sentences.

1. Ice cream is a frozen desert maded from milk and cream.

   _____

2. The first time a kone was used for surving ice cream was on 1904.

   _____

Complete the sentence with the correct word.

3. The biggest ice-cream _____ ever made weighed 24 tons!

                                sundae   Sunday

Complete the sentence with a possessive pronoun.

4. Is ice cream a favorite treat of _____?

Correct the sentences.

1. Can you name eny objex that are made of glass

   _____

2. Bottels baking dishes and windowes are all made of glass.

   _____

Write a coordinating conjunction to complete the compound sentence.

3. The Egyptians made glass, _____ the Romans were better at it.

Read the sentence to figure out the meaning of the bold word. Underline the meaning.

4. The first American glass **plant** was built in Jamestown, Virginia, in 1608.

   a place where things are made or built   a living thing

Correct the sentences.

1. more insects on Earth than any other kind of animal.

   _____

2. Most insects make our werld a better place to liv.

   _____

Read the sentence to figure out the meaning of the bold word. Write the meaning on the line.

3. Insects **benefit** us by eating the bugs that eat our plants.

   _____

Underline the words that do _not_ mean exactly what they say.

4. Although some insects bug us, most of them help us and our planet.

Correct the sentences.

1. In the book <u>charlotte's web</u>, a girl, a pig, and spider be friends.

   _____

2. The girls name is fern, The pigs name is wilbur, And the spiders name is charlotte.

   _____

Complete the sentence with the best word.

3. In the beginning of the story, Fern and Wilbur spend lots of time together

   _____ school.

   under   after

Add punctuation to the sentence.

4. In chapter 3, the author wrote Wilbur didn't want food, he wanted love

Read the bold word roots and their meanings. Notice the examples given for each root.

Word Roots	Meanings	Examples	
ped	foot	pedestrian	pedal
rupt	break	interrupt	erupt
tract	pull	tractor	attract
port	carry	portable	imported

Read the meaning of the word root. Complete the sentence with the word root that has that meaning.

1. **meaning:** break

   Please don't inter_____ me when I'm talking to your sister.

   meaning: pull

   The food on the picnic table is going to at_____ ants if we don't cover it.

   meaning: foot

   When _____estrians cross the street, drivers must stop to let them walk by.

   meaning: carry

   My mom's favorite tea is im_____ from China.

Write three sentences using three word roots from the box.

2. _____

   _____

3. _____

   _____

4. _____

   _____

Correct the sentences.

1. Puffins look kinda like penguins, but they are'nt penguins.

_____

2. Puffins have black and white fethers and ornj feet.

_____

Add punctuation to the sentence.

3. Puffins' beaks are a combination of the colors red yellow and blue

Underline the meaning of the bold word.

4. A puffin's beak is brightly colored in summer but **dull** in winter.

boring   not bright

Correct the sentences.

1. a lot of hard work, but building a treehouse can be fun.

_____

2. Before you begin, you has to plan careful.

_____

Rewrite the sentences to make a compound sentence.

3. A treehouse is built in the branches of a tree. Be sure to choose a sturdy tree.

_____

Complete the sentence with the correct homophone.

4. A treehouse can be made of _____ or some other material.

       wood   would

Correct the sentences.

1. The toy i like much is called legos.

   _____

2. legos are small plastick bloks that is used to build things.

   _____

Write a synonym for the bold word.

3. You can even **build** tall buildings with Legos. _____

Make the word *special* an adverb.

4. Legos come in many kinds of building sets for kids, and there are also sets

   special_____ made for adults.

Correct the sentences.

1. Raisins are a dryed and rinkled fruit.

   _____

2. Raisins are grapes that have been lefted in the son to dry.

   _____

Write the adverb that means *done by hand*.

3. Workers _____ pick the grapes and lay them on the ground.
   manually   quickly

Underline the preposition in the sentence.

4. Grapes don't become raisins until all the water inside them is removed.

Read the bold words and their definitions.

Words	Definitions
nation	a community of people with its own government
instrument	a tool that is used to do work
curiosity	wanting to know or learn something
display	a collection for others to see

Draw lines to match.

1. nation   wondering what it's like to visit the moon

   instrument   rock collection

   curiosity   United States

   display   ruler

Write a sentence using one of the bold words from the box.

2. _____

   _____

Correct the sentences.

1. The ostrich is the worlds larger bird.

   _____

2. This birds can't fly because they are too hevvy.

   _____

Read the sentences. Complete the second sentence with the word that means
***a made-up story*.**

3. Ostriches don't bury their heads in the sand. That is a _____.

                                                 myth   mystery

Complete the sentence with a reflexive pronoun.

4. An ostrich lies flat on the ground to protect _____ from danger.

Correct the sentences.

1. In may, 1776, a woman named Betsy Ross sowed the first American flag.

   _____

2. On June 14 1777, the Congress agreed on what the Flag would look like.

   _____

Underline the meaning of the bold word.

3. The first official **national** flag had thirteen stars.

   of or relating to a nation   of or relating to a colony

Underline the word that means *to put in order*.

4. The stars were arranged in a circle, in rows, or into one big star.

Correct the sentences.

1. Log kabins are an important part of histery.

_____

2. When people first settle in America, them used logs to build they houses.

_____

Underline the meaning of the bold word.

3. The people built the log cabins in wooded areas where trees were **plentiful**.

limited   more than enough

Complete the sentence with the best word.

4. The only _____ the pioneers used were an ax and a saw.

tools   machines

Correct the sentences.

1. A man invent roller skates, and her name was John Merlin.

_____

2. mr. Merlin wore them to a party and crash and fell.

_____

Write an antonym for the bold word.

3. Another man invented skates that only went **forward**. _____

Complete the sentence with an adverb.

4. _____, in 1863, a man invented skates that could turn.

Final   Finally

Read the bold word roots and their meaning in the shaded box. Then read the bold words and their definitions.

> **com** and **con** mean *together*
>
> **community**   a group of people living together in the same place
>
> **combine**   to bring or mix together
>
> **connect**   to join together

Write the word that best completes each sentence.

1. I like to _____ peanut butter and bananas, but my brother doesn't like those foods together.

2. My little sister likes to put paper tubes together and _____ them with string.

3. The town I live in is so small that I know most of the people in the _____.

Write a sentence using one of the bold words from the box.

4. _____

_____

Correct the sentences.

1. The orijinal purpose of the umbrella was to blok the sun.

_____

2. Originaly, people thought that umbrellas were only for womans.

_____

Add a suffix to make the adjective an adverb.

3. Men did not common_____ use umbrellas.

Complete the sentence with the best word.

4. After a man used an umbrella in 1756, umbrellas became

_____.

popular　　　pleasing　　　lovable

Correct the sentences.

1. Sea sponjes look like plants, but there animals.

_____

2. Near five thousand diffrent types live on the ocean flor.

_____

Complete the bold word with the root that means *together*.

3. Most sponges live their lives _____**nected** to a reef.

con　　　man　　　vis

Complete the sentence with a word that means *to grow again*.

4. If a piece of a sponge breaks off, the piece is able to _____.

Correct the sentences.

1. I haded to rite a book report for skool.

_____

2. For my report, I red <u>the mouse and the motorcycle</u>.

_____

Add punctuation to the sentence.

3. I wrote The story is about a mouse that lives in a hotel room.

Underline the verb phrase in the sentence.

4. "The story begins when Keith and his parents check in to the hotel."

Correct the sentences.

1. earth is surround by air.

_____

2. Air is needid by all liveing things on Earth.

_____

Complete the sentence with the correct homophone.

3. _____ and pollution create changes in the air.
   Whether   Weather

Complete the sentence with the correct word.

4. Polluted air can have harmful _____ on living creatures.
   effects   benefits

Read the bold words and their definitions.

Words	Definitions
demonstrate	to show how to do something
attempt	to try
respond	to answer; to say something in return
explain	to tell someone the reason for something; to make understandable

Write about a time when you demonstrated how to do something.

1. _____

_____

Write about a time when you attempted to do something.

2. _____

_____

Write about a time when you responded to someone.

3. _____

_____

Write about a time when you explained something to someone.

4. _____

_____

Correct the sentences.

1. Gotes are mounten animals that like to clime.

   _____

2. Them animals like to live in groops.

   _____

Complete the bold word with the root that is in the word *company*.

3. Goats like the company of other goats. They like to have goat _____**panions**.

Complete the sentence with the best word.

4. Goats will also _____ other kinds of animals as companions.

   get   accept   take

Correct the sentences.

1. Freindship Day is a first Sunday of august.

   _____

2. Childs in mine class make cards or pictures for his friends.

   _____

Add an apostrophe to make the bold word a possessive noun.

3. I wrote my two best **friends** names on a poster and decorated it.

Complete the sentence with the best word.

4. It's fun to do _____ things for people you care about.

   special   uncommon   pleasant

Correct the sentences.

1. Jupiter is covered in clouds, it's very windy there.

   _____

2. Jupiters' Great Red Spot is an storm that spinns around Jupiter.

   _____

Add a suffix to make the bold word a superlative adjective.

3. Jupiter is one of the **storm**_____ planets in the solar system.

Complete the sentence with the best word.

4. All of the other planets could fit inside Jupiter. Jupiter is _____!

               big   huge   full

Correct the sentences.

1. Won of the popularest holidays in America is halloween.

   _____

2. Halloween pumkins are usual orange, but they can also be green or wite.

   _____

Rewrite the sentences to make a complex sentence. Use a subordinating conjunction and a comma.

3. Halloween costumes are fun to wear. Most kids like to dress up.

   _____

Complete the bold word with a root that means *see*.

4. Last year I went as an **in**_____**ible** ghost.

Read the bold homophones and their meanings.

seas	large bodies of salt water; oceans
sees	uses his or her eyes; notices
seize	to take hold of in a sudden way

Write the homophone that best completes each sentence.

1. When my dog _____ me through the window, he barks at me.

2. Some frogs use their tongues to _____ their food.

3. The Red Sea is just one of the _____ on planet Earth.

Write a sentence using each homophone.

4. _____

_____

_____

_____

_____

_____

Correct the sentences.

1. Alligator's tungs cannot move.

_____

2. An alligator must rise their head to swallow food.

_____

Complete the sentence with the correct homophone.

3. Alligators use their sharp teeth to _____ and hold their food.

                          sees   seize   seas

Complete the sentence with a synonym for *safe*.

4. Alligators can walk on land, but they feel more _____ in water.

                          secure   daring   hungry

Correct the sentences.

1. Crocodiles have longer heds then alligators'.

_____

2. Crocodiles also have a more thin nose, and are a liter color.

_____

Underline the meaning of the bold word.

3. Alligators and crocodiles **spend** much of their time in the water.

to pay money for something   to allow time to pass

Underline the comparative adverb.

4. In the water, these animals are much faster than people.

Correct the sentences.

1. One of the most old toys in the world is the yo-yo.

   _____

2. The first modurn yo-yo comed to the United States in 1928.

   _____

Underline the preposition. Circle the adverb that tells where something is.

3. When the space shuttle *Atlantis* went into space, a yo-yo was taken aboard.

Make the bold word plural.

4. Today, there are several **compan**_____ that make and sell yo-yos.
                              ys   ies

Correct the sentences.

1. Lemmons have many intresting uses besides making lemon ade.

   _____

2. Some people use the leeves of a lemon tree, to make tee.

   _____

Add a comma to make a complex sentence.

3. When my mom makes chicken she bakes it with slices of lemon.

Circle the word root of the underlined word.

4. To write a message no one can see, use a lemon to make <u>invisible</u> ink.

Read the sentences. Think about what it's like to go to the beach.

> I like to go to the beach.
>
> I use a <u>shovel</u> to dig in the sand.
>
> I put seashells in my <u>pail</u>.
>
> My sister and I toss a <u>beach ball</u>
>
> back and forth.
>
> When the sand gets too hot,
>
> I put on my <u>sandals</u>.
>
> I lie on my <u>beach towel</u> and listen
>
> to the <u>waves</u>.

Read each bold word. Then write a similar word you would use to tell about the beach. Use the underlined words from above.

1. **basket** _____   **blanket** _____

   rain   _____   **rake** _____

   football _____   **rain boots** _____

Write the word or words that tell about playing on the beach.

2. I wear a _____ to protect my skin.
       sun hat   rain hat

3. I like to chase the _____.
       squirrels   sea gulls

Write a sentence about the beach. Use at least two of the words from the box.

4. _____

   _____

Correct the sentences.

1. Getting a good nights sleep can help you feel good and stay good.

_____

2. Sleep helps you brain work proper.

_____

Complete the bold word with a root that means _do_.

3. It seems like we don't do anything when we sleep, but the brain is very

_____**ive**.

Complete the bold word with a prefix that means _not_.

4. Our brains may be busy, but our muscles are _____**active**.

Correct the sentences.

1. Thief ants got their name because they steel other ants food.

_____

2. The ghost ant is hard to sea because of its pail color.

_____

Complete each sentence with the best word.

3. Red fire ants can hurt people with their _____ sting.

                              colorful   painful

4. Ants that smell bad are odorous ants. They have a bad _____.

                              flavor   odor   look

Correct the sentences.

1. Lots of the movies I seen have well stories about animals.

_____

2. Two characters from the movie <u>how to train your dragon</u> become heros.

_____

Underline the words that do *not* mean exactly what they say.

3. Mort from *Madagascar* drives everyone nuts because he's so cute and cuddly.

Underline the meaning of the bold word.

4. Scrat from *Ice Age* always hunts for his acorn so he can eat it or **bury** it.

   to hide in the ground   a small juicy fruit

Correct the sentences.

1. I got invited to a party for my bestest friend mike.

_____

2. The inviteation come in the male yesterday.

_____

Add punctuation to the sentence.

3. The invitation said Please come to a party for Mike's tenth birthday

Write the meaning of the underlined saying.

4. It also said, "Shh! The party is a surprise, so don't <u>spill the beans!</u>"

_____

Read the bold words and their similar meanings.

proud	very pleased by your achievements
satisfied	happy; content
self-assured	sure of yourself; confident

Write the word that best completes each sentence.

1. I felt _____ with the way my new soccer uniform fit me.

2. I was _____ when I scored a goal for my soccer team.

3. Coach said that we can win the game if we each play our best and are

   _____.

Write two sentences using two of the words from the box.

4. _____

   _____

   _____

   _____

My Progress

Week	Number Correct Each Day					Skill I Did Well	Skill I Need to Practice
	1	2	3	4	5		
1							
2							
3							
4							
5							
6							
7							
8							
9							
10							
11							
12							
13							
14							
15							
16							
17							
18							

My Progress (cont.)

Week	Number Correct Each Day					Skill I Did Well	Skill I Need to Practice
	1	2	3	4	5		
19							
20							
21							
22							
23							
24							
25							
26							
27							
28							
29							
30							
31							
32							
33							
34							
35							
36							

Daily Language Review • EMC 6823 • © Evan-Moor Corp.